Edward Pollock Anshutz

Dogs

How to Care for Them in Health and Treat Them When Ill

Edward Pollock Anshutz

Dogs

How to Care for Them in Health and Treat Them When Ill

ISBN/EAN: 9783845795058
Erscheinungsjahr: 2012
Erscheinungsort: Bremen, Deutschland

www.unikum-verlag.de | office@unikum-verlag.de

Bei diesem Titel handelt es sich um den Nachdruck eines historischen, lange vergriffenen Buches. Da elektronische Druckvorlagen für diese Titel nicht existieren, musste auf alte Vorlagen zurückgegriffen werden. Hieraus zwangsläufig resultierende Qualitätsverluste bitten wir zu entschuldigen.

Edward Pollock Anshutz

Dogs

How to Care for Them in Health and Treat Them When Ill

Dogs.

How to Care for Them in Health and Treat Them When Ill.

Homœopathic Treatment.

ILLUSTRATED.

COMPILED AND ARRANGED BY

E. P. ANSHUTZ.

PHILADELPHIA:
BOERICKE & TAFEL.
1903.

Seniors of the Pack.

CONTENTS.

We are two travellers, Roger and I.
  Roger's my dog—come here you scamp!
Jump for the gentleman—mind your eye!
  Over the table—look out for the lamp!
The rogue is growing a little old;
  Five years we've tramped through wind and weather,
And slept out of doors when nights were cold;
  And ate and drank and starved together.

The Vagabonds. *Trowbridge.*

PREFACE.

There have been many books published, large and small, on the treatment of the ills of dogs but none of them have been entirely successful. Some are too large and too learned for the average man and others too small and meagre. Every owner of a dog has a greater or less degree of affection for the animal, probably greater as is shown by the rough, but true, old maxim "never kick a dog unless you can lick his master"—and would gladly cure the dog when ill if he knew how and were not put to too great an expense. For such this book is designed—not for veterinarian but for the people who own dogs. It does not require any very great degree of medical lore to treat a sick dog and all that is requisite for the treatment of a large majority of cases will be found in this book plainly put and easily comprehended. A well-selected homœopathic remedy will act on a dog as on all animals, with marvelous rapidity and with wonderful benefit. The remedies cost but a trifle, and those in the family medicine chest will answer all purposes, as there is no need to give a horse, dog or cow any "stronger" medicine than is given to a baby.

Dr. Jas. T. Kent, of Chicago, has kindly revised this work and added much original matter to it.

Dogs in Health.

PERHAPS a very few preliminary remarks on the treatment of dogs in health may not be amiss here. Common sense, backed by kindness, will pretty well cover the whole ground in this particular; every one should realize this, but every one does not think of the matter in this light and it will do no harm to call attention to it. A dog is to a certain extent like a child, and a very little kindness and thoughtfulness will go a long ways with him.

Water.

For instance, reader, do you pay any attention to the subject of water for your dog?

Probably not; yet in this respect with the minimum of trouble to yourself you can give your dog the greatest boon possible. The following personal experience illustrates the point:

One summer, the writer was at a remote seaside resort—far from the maddening crowd and all that sort of thing. One day, two dogs came trotting up on the porch wagging their tails and generally conducting themselves as though they had come to scrape acquaintance. One was probably of the *genus* "cur" and we afterwards gave him the name "Jack," the other was a coach dog, left by his owner, and he was in time known as "Spot." The writer brought out a pan of good water and offered it to his guests, and it was evident that they appreciated the treat highly, for between them they emptied the pan, though it held about a quart. The next day both of them again appeared, and after a tail-wagging greeting, went over to the empty pan and then looked at their entertainer in a reproachfully questioning manner. The pan was at once refilled and afterwards kept filled at all times. The amount of water those two dogs drank was simply astonishing. One very hot day they both came rushing up on the porch, and Jack, without waiting to greet his entertainer, went for the pan at once and began drinking. Spot, who though much larger was always a follower of the rather diminutive, tow-colored Jack, stood by waiting his turn, but Jack did not cease till he had emptied the pan, and it had to be refilled for the other. In a very short time the two dogs made the porch their home. They were never given any food, nothing but water, and certainly, as the summer went on their condition materially improved. It seemed to prove pretty conclusively that to them the question of water was of more importance than food.

Food.

This must remain an open question as breeders and dog experts differ on it widely. Probably the common sense solution is to give the dog a change in food when convenient. Dogs are not gluttons, and a little wholesome food contents them. As a rule, pet dogs are fed too much. Puppies should be given a diet of milk, varied with bread and milk, or broth, and feed about once in three hours, until old enough to eat meat. But on all these points the owners of dogs are generally competent to decide what is best.

Took First Prize.

The bones, which dogs are fond of gnawing, are not gnawed from hunger but for the lime in them. The lime, it is affirmed by some authorities, is necessary for the health of the dog. The soft bones, such as the ribs of sheep and the small joints are the best for young dogs, as hard bones injure the teeth.

Sleeping Quarters.

When it is convenient the dog should have a dry and comfortable place that he can feel is his own for sleeping. Be assured the dog appreciates such a comfortable place as much, perhaps, as does a man. In summer it is not needed so much, but in winter and during the cold, raw seasons such a place is needed by the dog.

Homoeopathic Medicines.

HOMŒOPATHIC medicines are not "specific" to anything save the disease symptoms that are similar to those they will cause in the healthy; hence, it is that in each disease almost any medicine may be called for, as diseases are not entities but vary greatly in different individuals, though called by the same name. For example, one dog with a given named disease may seek warmth, shivering at any cold air, while another with the same disease, so far as the name goes, will seek cool air. Certainly the same remedy will not suit each case.

Strength.—Unless you are very familiar

with homœopathic remedies, ask for the "regular strength," *i. e.*, the third, in remedies like *Aconite*, etc., and the sixth, in others like *Arsenicum*, etc. And always remember that it is *not* the *quantity* of a drug that effects a cure, but its *homœopathicity* to the symptoms of the disease. The prevalent idea that if an infinitesimal dose will cure, a "stronger" one will do the work better, and quicker, is a *very* erroneous one. *Arsenicum*, or Arsenic, is a grand remedy, but if you take it too strong you get the poison effects. The sixth will give all of the curative effects and none of the evil effects.

Form of the Medicines.—Homœopathic remedies are prepared in several ways, *i. e.*, in pellet form, or as liquids or powders, and are equally efficacious in any of these three forms; use the form that is the most convenient. The pellet form, as a rule, is preferable, as pellets can be given dry on the tongue at any time.

Dose.—From 8 to 12 pellets, 5 drops of the liquid, of the powder, as much as will lie on the point of a pen-knife constitutes a dose, of the three forms respectively.

Frequency of the Dose.—In cases that are not acute give, as a general rule, from two to three doses every twenty-four hours. In acute cases a dose every two hours during the day is sufficient. When there is visible improvement, stop the medicine.

Keeping the Medicines.—Medicines should be kept well corked and in a dry, dark place. They may be purchased singly, but a case is to be preferred, as when you have a case or a medicine chest, you have them all and in one place. If you have a family medicine chest the medicines in it can be used, as there is no difference between them and those used in veterinary practice.

Administering the Medicines.—If given in pellets, if the dog will not lick them from your hand, open his mouth and drop them as far back on the tongue as possible. If liquids are used put the proper dose in a little water and the dog will usually lap it up at once; if not, open his mouth and put a spoonful of the water in his mouth.

For the Safety of the Public.

Diseases of Dogs.

Distemper.

OF all diseases to which dogs are subject, perhaps distemper is the most frequent, as it is also the most difficult to define. It has been compared to typhoid, or to typhus fever in man, though the comparison hardly seems to be a good one. The disease seems to be contagious. We say "seems to be," because back of all "contagious" diseases, in man or beast, is an element that no one can explain. Of a dozen men or dogs, exposed to a contagious disease a certain number may contract the disease while the remainder, though equally exposed, will escape. When we are able to explain this we will know more of "contagious" diseases than we do now. However, distemper is to be mechanically classed as a contagious disease.

It is more apt to attack young dogs, and those known as "pure breed," than old dogs and the dog rabble, but at any rate if a dog shows signs of the disease it is best to isolate him from the other dogs, if any be kept, about the place. The symptoms of the disease vary considerably. The following is the picture of it drawn by Blaine:

"One of the earliest symptoms is a short, dry, husky cough, which is followed by a lessening of the appetite, of the flesh, strength, and spirits; the coat also begins to stare, and the eyes to wink in a full light, as though painfully affected by it; they also, if observed in the morning, exhibit the remains of a little hardened mucus, which may be seen adhering to the inner corner of each, while a general cloudiness of the eye steals over its surface; the nose also is bedewed with a watery discharge, greater or less as the membranous linings of the orbits and nasal cavities are more or less inflamed, in which state it may sometimes remain for two or three weeks without much alteration; it eventually, however, increases, and changes from a limpid watery fluid to a muco-purulent discharge (something like the discharge from an abscess), which flows down the face from the inner corner of each eye, and as the disease becomes more intense it frequently closes up the lids during the night, and blinds the dog until his efforts have opened them. The nasal discharge, which is at first thin and watery, becomes muco-purulent, and next one of direct pus, by which his nose is no less closed up each morning by the viscid exudations his eyes. As the intensity of the inflammation extends, the cough also, which was at first a slight huskiness (or perhaps hardly existed at all, for in some cases but little cough attended the early stages), increases to a distressing, harsh-sounding, and frequent attempt to forcing something up the throat by an effort that appears compounded of coughing and vomiting. To these appearances are usually added wasting, weakness, listlessness and lessening of the appetite also."

Remembering that dogs cannot relate their symptoms, or feelings, we would be inclined to regard the foregoing as being nearer to grippe than to typhoid, or typhus.

Of this disease Hurndall says: "I look upon distemper as a catarrhal fever, affecting, more or less severely, the mucous membranes of the various canals of the body, the nervous system being not infrequently implicated."

Lord says: "A contagious disease of which all dogs appear to carry the seeds in their system, accompanied with fever and derangement of most of the internal organs, and frequently ending in chorea, paralysis or inflammation of the lungs." If the seeds of the disease are in the system it can hardly be termed a contagious disease.

Moore says: "The symptoms present considerable variations, which depend upon the rapidity of the disease, the character of the prevailing epidemic, and the local complication."

Mills after stating that the symptoms are very numerous and varied, concludes that "it will not be feasible to enumerate all the combinations that occur, as these are simply endless." From the foregoing, the reader will see that "distemper," the worst of dog diseases, is a rather meaningless term, and that the only way to intelligently treat the disease is to individualize the cases, *i. e.*, do not think of the *name* of the disease, but look for the symptoms in the dog.

At the onset, if the dog is feverish, or chilly and feverish by turns, and restless, give him *Aconite*, as this great polychrest arrests more diseases in their incipiency than any other remedy.

Or, should the dog appear dull, feverish and stupid, "drunken looking," give him *Gelsemium.* The difference between the two is, that *Aconite* has restlessness prominent, while *Gelsemium* is characterized by a dull, sluggish, besotted condition. These two, *Aconite* and *Gelsemium*, are only of use in the beginning

A Scrap.

of the disease. If they do not check it resort must be had to others as indicated.

Bryonia will be called for when the dog has symptoms of bronchitis, which is known by short, hurried breathing, as though the act were painful, together with rattling of mucus, a short dry cough, which may become moist and loose, with blood streaked mucus. When the mucus becomes "rusty" instead of being blood streaked then should *Phosphorus* be given. A dangerous stage.

Where a *clear* fluid runs from the nose and eyes, either or both, and that symptom is very prominent, accompained, it may be, by fever and the other symptoms, *Natrum mur.* will be indicated.

When there is diarrhœa and exhaustion, *i. e.* when the vital powers seem to sink, offensive and acrid effusion from inflamed nose and eyes, with great restlessness and constant whining, then *Arsenicum* will be called for.

Should the mouth be more or less ulcerated, breath peculiarily offensive, with bloody diarrhœa, *Mercurius* must be given.

Belladonna is called for especially when the throat is inflamed and the eyes involved; also, when the brain seems to be involved and there are "fits."

Many readers, however, may know that their dog has "distemper" and yet not be able to, or have the time to, differentiate between the various remedies. To these we would say, give him *Arsenicum* for a few days and then follow with *Nux vomica.* Indeed the majority of cases will yield to this treatment.

Allopathic writers lay great stress on feeding in this disease, and state that every means should be employed to induce the dog to eat so as to "sustain his strength." This, we think, is a mistake. Give the dog access to plenty of pure water, but do not try to force him to eat. He is like a sick man, it may be, to whom the very thought of food is disgusting. Cure the *disease* by the indicated remedy, and nature will soon supply the appetite when the disease is conquered.

Influenza.

This disease so closely resembles distemper in dogs that practically there is no difference between them—the difference, probably, between "grippe" and influenza. It is indicated by altered breathing, sneezing, fever and prostration; watering eyes and nose.

Aconite, as a rule, at the beginning, will cut the trouble short. If it does not then resort to

Nux vomica, especially if there be constipation or to *Arsenicum* if discharges take on a purulent character.

Laryngitis.

This disease, in common parlance, is a croupy sore throat—larynx inflamed, with difficulty in swallowing.

Belladonna is probably the best remedy, especially if there is an alteration in the dog's voice and cough, these with undoubted inflammation of the throat; or should it be especially noticeable that the dog is averse to motion, wants to remain quiet, then *Bryonia* will be the better remedy. *Belladonna* is more for acute inflammatory states and rather excitable and feverish conditions, such as are noticeable in eyes and demeanor.

Pleurisy, Pneumonia.

Pleurisy is simply an inflammation of the pleura, and the pleura is the membrane lining the chest. If there is much effusion the disease is very dangerous. The dog exhibits evidence of pain and has quick short breath.

Pneumonia is an inflammation of the lungs themselves. A dog suffering from pneumonia has great difficulty in breathing; inflamed eyes, generally dry and hot nose, sits on his haunches with extended head and open mouth and does not rest easy when he lies down. Pleurisy has repeated chills, while in pneumonia there is only one; also, in the latter there is generally the "rust colored" sputa. Pleurisy has "stitching" pains, while pneumonia is simply (as the word in the Greek shows) difficult breath.

If there is reason to suspect that the case is one of pneumonia, *Aconite* will be a good first prescription, and, indeed, it will also cover the case should it be pleurisy. It is indicated by high fever, short breath and oppressed breathing of pneumonia and by the same general symptoms in pleurisy, with its catchy breath, pain on inhalation and short cough. As the case progresses, *Bryonia* may be given with advantage as an intercurrent remedy.

Fevers.

Fevers may be brought on by many causes —sudden change in temperature, jumping in cold water when over-heated, unusually violent exercise, etc.

The eyes are red, swollen and watery, the pulse rapid, the nose dry and hot, hot mouth,

3 In Full Chase.

thirst and restlessness. The dog gets up, turns around, lies down again, yet has a drowsy, or anxious look.

Aconite given every hour will, as a rule, quickly terminate the attack.

If dog's eyes are unnaturally bright and he seems delirious give *Belladonna.*

If heat becomes burning, there is great prostration, constant thirst, nose and tongue dry and cracked, *Arsenicum* is the remedy.

Where the fever is caused by an injury of any sort, *Arnica* should be used.

Asthma.

This is a complaint that affects old dogs chiefly, as the young ones are not often affected by it. Asthma is easily recognized by the labored, wheezy, loud breathing, the panting for breath that is not caused by violent exertion; the appetite is not often impaired, but the breath is apt to be bad and coat rough and almost mangy looking.

Ipecacuanha is a remedy for asthma that comes on in spasms with rattling of mucus in chest and tendency to vomit.

Nux vomica is suitable for asthma associated with indigestion, and *Arsenicum* when the attacks abate on coughing up some mucus.

The following by Dr. Robert T. Cooper, in the *Homœopathic Review* is interesting in this connection though the case was not precisely one of asthma:

"It can hardly be supposed to interest the readers of the *Homœopathic Review* to know that I possess in my dog a fidus Achates, but when I inform them that this dog has witnessed the suns of fifteen summers, and that calculating a year of dog's life to be equivalent to (at least) five of a man's, my dog must be a patriarch; and since, moreover, I am given to understand that my dog is, with his sister (supposing her earthly existence unterminated), the last of his breed—the loup-loup breed, an extinct variety of dog—their interest cannot fail to be roused. But the entertainment will, I doubt not, be still further enhanced when I declare that the combined influence of antiquity and obesity combine to make a dog pant, the best laid schemes of dogs and men "gang aft a-gley," and panting continues until death parts breathing and dog. And so I thought it would be with my dog, till a friend informed me of a canine fancier in Dublin who cured all such difficulties with *Bryonia.* Accordingly I procured some special pilules of *Bryonia*, third decimal, and gave him a few doses, three or four at a time of these agreeable medicaments, and was surprised to find in a week or two a most noticeable difference in the breathing of my valued quadruped."

"The improvement was not due to suggestion either; for although I have a very good opinion of my dog's intelligence, this belief is not such as would lead me to ascribe to him a susceptibility to the influence of this newest method of treatment. He is, naturally a believer in drugs, when the bases of these consist of sugar of milk, and he evidently does not require any suggestion to make the remedy tell with full effect. While this pulmono-cardiac canine regeneration was proceeding, a lady of seventy-two asked me to prescribe something for her panting breathing; after walking a short distance continued panting comes on, and when she enters a shop she has to sit down and remain silent a minute or two, notwithstanding the polite bow and 'what may I show you, madam,' of the disposer of merchandise."

I had no difficulty in assuring my lady friend that all she required was to be treated like a dog, and like a dog she was treated, with the results that the second dose of *Bryonia*, third decimal, relieved her breathing."

Cold, Coryza, Catarrh, Ozaena.

If the dog gets a "common cold," *i. e.*, sneezes, is a little feverish, "runs" at the nose and this state is noticed in time a few doses of *Aconite* will quickly cure.

A form of catarrh will often follow distemper, or a dog will be affected with a species of catarrh, the same as a human being. Where

HAVING SOME FUN.

the trouble is the sequel of distemper, *Kali mur.* will give more satisfaction, perhaps, than any other remedy. It is a remedy especially suitable for secondary forms of disease, especially of the lungs or nose.

Should the catarrh take the form known as ozæna, in which the discharge is purulent, fetid and more or less bloody, the remedies called for are *Aurum*, or *Kali phos.* It is difficult to give the differentiation between these two remedies unless it be that *Aurum* is called for when there is reason to believe that the bones are involved, and *Kali phos.* where the condition of the system is depraved and the discharges are peculiarly foul.

Rheumatism.

Dogs, especially house-dogs, are nearly as

much subject to rheumatism as their masters. And the disease is from the same cause—wet and cold.

The shoulders and legs are stiff, and the animal often limps, or holds up one paw and shows evidence of pain, even howling sometimes when he puts the paw down. The breathing may be accelerated. Affected parts are tender to the touch.

Aconite is the first remedy for the feverish state.

Rhus tox. where there is great stiffness, swollen joints, great tenderness, and worse when beginning to move. This remedy will probably cure more cases than any other. Give it every two hours.

Bryonia is especially indicated when the animal evinces great disinclination to move. The *Rhus* case on the contrary is restless, apparently the pain causing him to move, while the *Bryonia* case only feels the pain acutely when moving.

Another remedy to be considered is *Dulcamara*, which should be given in cases where every cold, damp day the dog shows signs of rheumatic pains.

In cases where the pain is not so much in evidence, in what might be termed chronic rheumatism, *Sulphur* once a day is the remedy. *Nux vomica* can also be considered.

In a German Journal there is a case related of a Newfoundland dog who rescued a child from icy water. The boy was none the worse from his icy bath, but "the dog sickened and was in pain. He would drag himself along, taking little notice of anyone even though petted. Four or five times daily he was beset with cramps, always when moving about; the dog would then stand still and wince, his hind legs would twitch, and he would alternately raise one and then the other, the embrocations and liniments of the veterinarian proving of no avail. *Belladonna* and then *Cocculus* were administered, but the hoped for relief did not come. The dog was failing fast when at last *Nux vomica* 3 was administered, one dose a day, and after eight doses the dog was cured, barring a slight lameness. In other respects the dog is in as good spirits and as healthy as before."

The following case was reported by a correspondent of *Leip. Pop. Z. fuer Hom.*:

The Royal Forrester Luban, of Burg, wrote: 'My Skye terrier, Romeo, which I may mention is of very great value, having been bought by me two years ago for 600 marks, has been suffering four weeks with rheumatism. Symptoms: He will suddenly writhe, raise up his back high and remain standing with his head hanging down and moaning. If he is even touched, he will cry out aloud. The pulse beats high, the heartbeat is irregular, the jugular artery swells up and you can see the blood rushing through it. Put into his kennel, the dog will remain in this position, hold up his left forefoot for about ten minutes. Then he will lie down for a long time, very much exhausted,' *Aconite*, *Bryonia* and *Rhus* did no good. E. K. diagnosed the case to be rheumatism of the heart and prescribed *Cactus grand.* and *Kalmia lat.*, which completely cured in two weeks' time, and the dog took first prize at the kennel show at Dusseldorf.

The following case is related by Dr. Maench:

A superb setter dog, warm from exertion, jumped into a cold stream and for nearly a year had been apparently hopelessly lame, notwithstanding all the efforts of the allopathic veterinarians. "The dog seemed to be worse when trying to get up from his bed. He would yelp and howl from pain, and turn and twist pitifully till he gained his legs. The small of the back must be lame for he waddled when walking, especially at first, and when trying to rise, his hind legs for a time drag on the floor. As no one seemed able to help him he would have been shot, but for his being so excellent a hunter. He was given *Rhus tox.*, morning and evening. 'About a week later a fine setter trotted past me, and a hundred yards behind him I encountered Mr. B. On inquiry the dog proved to be the one who a week before was given the *Rhus tox.* The little pellets had worked like magic.'"

A Life Saver.

Sore Throat.

This may be recognized by sneezing, hoarse cough and noisy breathing, and the hot inflamed appearance of the throat. On grasping the dog's throat between the thumb and finger, the dog will give evidence of pain and often a lump may be felt.

Belladonna is the first and best remedy, every half hour.

Spongia for noisy breathing.

If case gets no better give *Hepar sulph.*

Mr. Joseph Borkhalder, V. S., related this case in *Homœopathic Recorder*: "A dog was brought to me which had not eaten anything for four days and could not swallow. I prescribed *Belladonna* and *Mercurius*, to be given alternately every two hours. In four days the dog was as well as ever."

Coughing.

Coughing, as a rule, is a mere symptom of some other disease. But if there is no apparent disease the cough may be treated as follows:

Dry, convulsive, and especially if in evidence at night, give *Belladonna.*

Caused by cold, damp weather, *Dulcamara.*

With rattling of mucus, gagging or vomiting, *Ipecacuanha.*

Short, dry, frequent, *Aconite.*

When cough is seemingly very painful, *Bryonia.*

Diarrhoea.

Where evacuations are bloody and there is

evident straining, *Mercurius* is indicated, every two hours.

With great thirst, foul evacuations, debility and trembling of the limbs, *Arsenicum.*

Colic, gripes, with slimy evacuation and pains coming at regular intervals, *Colocynth.*

Sulphur will follow well after any of the above named remedies and will often cure when the others have failed, and is the proper remedy when other remedies have only partially cured.

The following case was reported by Dr. Jas. T. Kent, owner of a number of fine dogs, in *Journal of Homœopathics:*

"Belva, an Irish water spaniel, was taken suddenly with dysentery. Stools bloody, slimy, frequent, scanty. She would strain as if she could not finish the stool and pass but a small gob of mucus mixed with blood. She was given *Mercurius* and quickly cured."

4

The straining, frequent, scanty and bloody stools, were here the guide to the remedy.

Dr. Kallenbach, of Utrecht, relates the case of a fine poodle dog that would be attacked two or three times a day with spasms in the abdomen, during which it would roll about the floor, uttering pitiful cries and sometimes ending in downright convulsions. Veterinarians said the sickness, an ulceration of the bowels as in chronic typhus, was incurable. "I gave the dog, as a matter of experiment four doses of *Arsenicum*, after which two more of the spasmodic attacks occurred. Then he was given four more doses of that remedy, which completed the cure, and the dog is in good health yet. Five years later I cured another case of this disease with the same remedy."

Constipation.

Caused by improper food, lack of exercise or liver disease.

Nux vomica for a few days followed by *Sulphur* every two hours will generally effect a cure.

For old fat dogs give *Opium.*

When accompanied with pain give *Plumbum.*

Prolonged straining to pass a soft or normal stool, *Alumina.*

Worms.

Dogs are very subject to worms, which are passed with the feces and at times are vomited. Their presence may be determined by the general irritability, restlessness, unsociability, variable appetite, and offensive breath.

Cina will cure most cases.

Sulphur is a good remedy to finish with.

For round worms, *Santonine.*

For pinworms, *Sabadilla.*

The dog often drags himself across the floor on his hinder parts to scratch the anus ; a sure sign of pinworms. *Sabadilla* will often cure.

Liver Disease.

May be caused by cold, damp weather or extremely hot weather; also want of exercise.

May be diagnosed by the vomiting of yellowish, or greenish fluid, general yellowish appearance of dog about the eyes and skin, loss of appetite and desire for solitude.

Nux vomica is the remedy for house dogs,

Scotch Collie "Eclipse."

especially if the disease is accompanied with constipation.

Mercurius for yellow and dirty appearance. If these fail give *Natrum sulph.*

Vomiting.

Usually it is nature's means of relieving the stomach of some substance that disagrees and it signifies nothing more, unless it be persistent.

Violent vomiting and retching calls for *Ipecacuanha.*

Vomiting of bile, constipation, *Nux vomica.* This remedy is especially adapted to house dogs.

Vomiting of green slime, with drooling, *Natrum sulph.*

Long standing cases when every drink of

water is vomited as soon as it reaches the stomach, with debility and emaciation, *Arsenicum.*

With total loss of appetite, *Antimonium crud.*

E. C. Sayre, V. S., reported the following case in *Americian Veterinary Review:* A small terrier had been vomiting for several days. The only peculiar thing about it is that every time it drank it induced vomiting, and there was great thirst. This I thought was a clear case for *Arsenic*, for we find in the proving of *Arsenicum*: 'Great thirst, vomiting, aggravated by drinking cold water.' I gave *Arsenicum*, but to my surprise was telephoned for the next day to call and see the dog which had not improved. On careful questioning I found that the vomiting did not occur until about fifteen minutes after drinking. In the proving of *Phosphorus* we find: 'Great thirst, vomiting of water as soon as it gets warm in the stomach.' *Phosphorus* was given, and that was the last of the vomiting."

This case shows the precision of homœopathic remedies and the necessity of a thorough acquaintance with the homœopathic materia medica.

Haematuria.

This means blood in the urine, which may occur from a variety of causes.

Cantharis every two hours will cure.

Nephritis.

Nephritis is inflammation of the kidneys. It is not a common disease, but dangerous.

It may be brought on by wet or cold, over-exertion, or strain.

The loins are tender, the hind legs stiff and carried wide apart; mouth and nose, dry and hot; thirst; urine passed with difficulty and in small quantities, high colored; appetite gone; disinclination to move, though dog is apt to turn his head to look at his loins, the seat of the pain.

Aconite is the remedy for the first stages of the disease as indicated by the fever, thirst, etc.

Cantharis comes in when urine is voided with difficulty, only a few drops at a time; bloody.

If urine is passed very bloody, *Terebinthina* is the remedy.

If the disease is caused by over-exertion, *Arnica* can be given as an intercurrent with benefit.

The following clinical case appeared in *Homœopathic Recorder:*

"A young dog, the property of E. was thrown into a pond while the water was cold; in consequence the animal caught a terrific cold, some force of which seemed to spend itself upon the kidneys. Upon visiting the canine patient, the animal was found to be feverish, the posterior parts stiff apparently from the manner in which it dragged itself about; the lumbar region upon pressure seemed painful, the urine was passed with pain and strangury, it being of a darker color, more concentrated and bloody somewhat at times, especially after the disease had progressed a few days. The stools were passed at long intervals and were dry and hard."

"As the disease process had begun apparently from the wetting *Aconite* was given every

A San Bernard.

half-hour, in water. The animal was well covered and given soft unirritating food, fresh drinking water and kept in a well protected place. The *Aconite* ameliorated the primary symptoms somewhat and was continued to be given. Finally the slight hæmaturia appearing *Cantharis* was given in alternation, which two medicines together in the course of about ten days led to a cure."

Cystitis.

This disease is an inflammation of the bladder.

It is caused by exposure to wet or cold, or may be brought on by violent exercise after dog has been tied up for several days.

The symptoms are ineffectual attempts to pass water, and what does pass is apt to be clouded and discharge usually ends with a few drops of pus. Hind legs tremble and belly is hot and distended.

Belladonna given every half-hour will cure most cases. But if case shows no signs of improvement then change to *Cannabis sat.*

Gonorrhoea, Balanitis.

An inflammation of the glans penis and mucous lining of prepuce, caused by uncleanliness, infection or excessive coition.

It is shown by constant discharge of matter.

Give *Mercurius* every three or four hours while discharge continues, *Cantharis* if discharge of urine is difficult. Wash parts with warm water containing some tincture of *Calendula*, about a tablespoonful to the pint.

Gleet, which is a chronic gonorrhœa, characterized by discharge of thick yellow or white mucus, also requires *Mercurius.*

Arsenicum and *Thuja* have also been used in the treatment of this disease.

Inflammation of the Teats.

This occurs generally a few days after the pups are born and if it is not arrested suppuration may take place. It is often so painful that the mother will not suckle the pups.

Aconite every two hours will generally give prompt relief. If no better after the first day give *Phytolacca.*

A meat diet should not be given during the continuance of the disease.

Boils.

For boils appearing on any part of the body

Hepar sulph. is the remedy; after they have opened change to *Silicea.*

Parasites.

The only way to free a dog from fleas or lice is to kill the parasites. Wash dog thoroughly and rub him with *Sulphur ointment* or *Crealine* in weak solution. Also see to it that his old bedding is destroyed and the kennel thoroughly disinfected. Internally give *Sulphur.*

Mange.

Mange is a species of itch. The hair comes off in patches and skin is dry and scaly, with red spots, and the animal is always scratching itself. Internally give the dog *Sulphur* and wash him thoroughly and rub the affected parts with *Sulphur ointment.*

Sepia for dry mange.

Arsenicum for scabby, red and inflamed sores.

In Homœopathy diseases are recognized by name for the sake of convenience only, for the same disease *by name* may require different remedies according to symptoms as is evidenced by the two following cases of mange reported by Professor J. T. Kent, in *Journal of Homœopathics*, which shows that the symptoms must govern the choice of a remedy.

"Jennie L., English setter bitch, was affected with mange in patches here and there on the sides and belly. She wanted to lie near the grate, dreaded the cold, open air, and would whine when washed. Got *Hepar sulph.* and soon recovered."

"Max, English setter dog, took mange. It began under the jaws and spread down the neck and there were patches on the belly. He was sensitive to heat, would lie under an open window, and wanted to be out of doors; he would go under the hydrant when water was running. He got *Pulsatilla* and rapidly recovered, and remained well for some time. It started up again and more *Pulsatilla* cured him permanently."

The first remedy was selected because the dog was averse to cold and to water, while the other wanted both. Two true homœopathic cases.

Sore Feet.

When paws are painful, swollen and bleeding from hard running or any external cause wash them clean and apply a lotion of *Arnica tincture*, one part of *Arnica* to twenty parts water. If suppurating apply pure *Succus*

On Guard.

Calendulæ. Rest, of course, is essential. If feverish give *Aconite* internally. When suppuration sets in give *Hepar sulph.*, every two hours.

Burns or Scalds.

Burns or scalds are best treated by applying the tincture of *Urtica urens.*

Abscesses and Tumors.

An abscess is a swelling, hot and inflamed that increases in size until it bursts and matter is discharged.

If attended with much fever give *Aconite.*

Hepar sulph. will hasten the ripening of the abscess.

After abscess has burst give *Silicea* to hasten healing.

There are two species of tumors, hard tumors (indurated), and the sac or bag, (encysted). Neither are painful. They are caused by wounds, bruises, or heredity.

Hard tumors can be cut out, or if this be undesirable, give internally *Phytolacca* every day; if this fails give *Calcarea fluor.*

Encysted tumors can be opened and let the contents escape. If they are the direct result of a blow, *Arnica* internally will sometimes remove them. *Silicea* is the remedy to be given internally for encysted tumors not the result of injury. If there is excessive heat and burning give a few doses of *Arsenicum.*

Apoplexy.

Over-fed house dogs like over fed men are subject to attacks of apoplexy. The dog staggers, the muscles twitch and he falls unconscious.

Exercise and less food are the means by which this disease may be prevented.

At the onset of the attack give *Aconite* every fifteen minutes.

Belladonna if the legs and body jerk.

Apis for total unconsciousness and heavy, noisy breathing.

Paralysis.

Total or partial loss of muscular power in any part of the body. Its cause is obscure —brain disease, injury or following other diseases. It must not be confused with rheumatism; of this however there is little danger if it be observed that in paralysis there is no inflammation.

Nux vomica is the remedy for the majority of cases. This failing try *Rhus tox*, two doses a day.

Epilepsy.

Epilepsy or "fits" may come from a variety of causes, such as heredity, worms, eating to much raw flesh, etc.

The dog falls to the ground, yelps, struggles, froths, etc.; in fact a regular "fit."

Belladonna is the remedy during the attack; give several doses in quick succession.

Nux vomica will do well as a preventive of future attacks; give once a day for a few weeks.

If caused by worms *Cina* is the remedy.

For involuntary twitchings of the muscles (chorea) give *Belladonna*.

Ophthalmia.

Ophthalmia, sore eyes; eyelids and eyeballs inflamed.

The disease may originate from a variety of causes, *i. e.*, injuries, change of temperature, etc.

The eyes are very sensitive to the light, they water or discharge mucus, or are glued together.

Aconite on first sign of inflammation will abort the disease. Every half hour a dose.

If relief does not follow soon give *Belladonna.*

For profuse watering of the eyes give *Euphrasia.*

Discharge of mucus, eyes glued shut, *Mercurius* every two hours.

When more violent symptoms subside give

a dose of *Sulphur* daily for two or three days.

If caused by a blow give *Arnica.*

Wash the eyes with tepid water.

Dr. H. Fisher, (*Zeitschr.· für Hom. Thier.*) gives the following concerning this disease:

"In such cases I have the eyes washed with *Euphrasia*—forty drops of the tincture in half a pint of lukewarm water—three times daily. Internally I give *Sulphur* with *Euphrasia* every two hours and have, even in the worst cases, cured the disease."

Fistula Lachrymalis.

Fistula lachrymalis is evidenced by tears or pus running from the dog's eyes. It is caused by some obstruction of the ducts, which in time is forced out, leaving a fistulous opening.

Silicea and *Calcarea carb.* are the remedies.

Try the first named daily for ten days, when, if no improvement, try the other.

Cataract.

Cataract is opacity of the crystalline lens, causing blindness. The cause is obscure, but seems to be mostly from old age, though not always. Homœopathic remedies have cured many cases in man and beast.

Calcarea fluorica is the remedy that seems to cure more cases than any other remedy. Give it once a day.

Cannabis sativa has also cured some cases.

The following case was reported by B. von Reichberger:

"I recently made a fine cure in a magnificent Newfoundland dog. A friend possesses such a dog and is fairly crazy about him. About four weeks ago I visited him and found him

The Puppy Show.

quite despondent; his favorite Pluto had become blind. I examined the dog and found a dense white covering over both eyes; he was stone blind. On inquiry I was told that Pluto had a festering sore on the head which was very much inflamed for several days. Presently the eyes became inflamed also, and the animal became blind in both eyes. I comforted the owner, assuring him that his dog would regain eyesight inside of a week. I prescribed once every two hours, two drops of the first dilution of *Cannabis sativa* in a teaspoonful of water and, at the same time, a few drops of this mixture between the separated eyelids every two hours. On the third day the dog began to see, for though the eyes still looked opaque he walked everywhere. In five days the eyes were as clear as ever, not a trace of the opacity remaining. As Pluto was a well-known and favored personality in the whole town this cure created much surprise."

Inflammation of the Ear.

An inflammation of the inner ear ending in an offensive discharge.

It may be recognized by the dog shaking his head, rubbing the ear against something and howling from pain.

Belladonna is the first remedy, every half hour.

When discharge sets in give *Mercurius* twice a day.

If dog be weak and discharge is excoriating give *Arsenicum.*

For scurfy ears give *Sulphur* once a day, or *Arsenicum* if scurf is scaly and the ears hot.

Bronchocele.

This is an enlargement of the thyroid gland recognized by an enlargement of the neck without inflammation or redness. It is also known as goitre and wen.

These hard swellings are often difficult to trace both in man and beast. *Calcarea fluor.* has perhaps, cured more of such cases than any other remedy; it is especially indicated when the swelling is notably hard.

Warts.

Warts may grow on any part of the body. Cutting them out does not free the system from its warty condition; this can only be done by internal medication, and the best remedy to do it with is *Thuja*—and in a rather high potency, say, the 30th. It may be well to give as an intercurrent remedy a dose of *Sulphur* occasionally, also of a rather high potency, if the remedy does not seem to act after a week or two.

Thuja is Hahnemann's "sycotic" remedy, and the warts for which it is especially indicated are those of a moist, fig-like or cauliflower nature.

Causticum is also a remedy of unusual value in the treatment of warts, as is also *Calcarea carb.*

Don't burn, cauterize or excise the warts from a dog; it is a cruel and useless proceeding, though in harmony with the growing error that to cut away the visible evidence of a diseased state and to lull or suppress its pain is the chief end of medicine. True medicine reaches the constitutional cause of a disease, and removing that the man or beast is made sound. But this condition is not reached by the use of the knife or external means.

Slobbering.

If the dog slobbers to an unusual extent give him a dose or two of *Mercurius*, which will be especially indicated if the mouth be in an unhealthy condition.

Canker in the Mouth.

Recognized by swollen gums, " proud flesh," and discharge of bloody and offensive matter. The best remedy is *Mercurius*, once a day. This failing try *Calcarea carb.*, *Carbo veg.*, or *Nitric acid.*

Teeth.

Should a young dog's teeth decay unnaturally a few doses of *Kreosotum* will arrest the trouble.

Should you have reason to believe that the dog suffers from toothache *Mercurius* will give him ease, though should you be able to definitely locate the trouble and find the tooth, or gums hot and swollen, *Aconite* would be the better remedy.

Inflammation of the Tongue.

Should the tongue become inflamed, which sometimes occurs, rendering swallowing extremely difficult, give the dog *Aconite*, and this failing to give prompt relief resort to *Belladonna.*

Where a vesicular eruption appears on the tongue give *Mercurius.*

Wounds.

Surgical treatment is beyond the scope of this book and should such treatment be required it is best to call in a veterinarian. However, Homœopathy can give great aid in the treatment of wounds of many sorts.

Arnica. For the ill effects of blows, contusions, falls, etc., *Arnica* is the remedy. Apply the tincture, diluted, one part tincture to twenty parts water, to the hurt place, and give the potentized *Arnica* internally. Where there is no evidence of injury externally, yet the dog evidently feels the effects of it, give *Arnica* 3 internally.

Calendula. This is the remedy for bleed-

POINTING.

ing wounds. Use the tincture, or, better still, the *Succus Calendulæ*, diluted one-half with water. It heals all raw or bleeding surfaces with marvelous rapidity and prevents suppuration.

Ledum. This is the remedy for all *punctured* wounds. Apply *Ledum* tincture, diluted with two parts water, externally to the wound and at the same time give *Ledum* 3 internally.

The following, illustrating the use of *Ledum*, appeared in the *Medical Advance*, being a report of the discussion of the meeting of a homœopathic medical society:

Dr. Kent: I have just one dog story. The dog belonged to John Belcher. This dog became too much interested in a cow that was going through the process of labor. The dog persisted in his attentions until the cow turned on him and hooked him through the hind leg. It was a punctured wound and stiffness followed its healing, so he was no longer able to pose as a ten thousand dollar dog. It seemed to be chronic stiffness and induration. I sent a dose of *Ledum*, which restored him to usefulness and his proper place as a prize dog. I understand his price has risen since.

Materia Medica.

THE following is a concise enumeration of the leading indications for the chief remedies named in this book:

Aconite.—Restlessness, anxiety, fear, shivering, alternating with fever. Inflammation, congestion, fever. Skin, or nose, hot and dry. A remedy suitable at the beginning of nearly all acute diseases.

Antimonium crudum.—Irritable, tongue white, dislikes being in the sun. Poor appetite. Hot swelling of knee joints. Callous excrescences. Excoriated nostrils. Disordered stomach.

Apis.—Inflammatory conditions of urinary organs. Dropsy. No thirst. Puffy swellings. Sudden starts in sleep. Avoids warm room.

Arnica.—Useful, internally and externally, for effects of blows, concussions, shocks and excessive exertion.

Arsenicum. — Prostration, burning pain, great thirst. Scaly, scurfy skin. Seeks warm places. Acrid, excoriating discharges. Wasting away. Evacuations dark and offensive. In case dog has been bitten by another dog give **Arsenicum.**

Aurum metallicum.—Foul ulcerations; discharge of fetid matter from the nose. Ozæna. Diseases attacking the bones.

Belladonna.—Unnaturally bright eyes, wild look, pupils dilated. Eyes inflamed. Throat red and swollen—sore throat; difficulty in swallowing. Convulsive movements. Mouth hot, skin red and hot. Red rashes. Hot throbbings.

Bryonia.—Oppressed breathing, difficult and painful. Remains quiet, worse on motion. Tenderness of parts to the touch. Constipation. Rheumatism. Pneumonia and inflammatory state of lungs and pleura. Cough dry and painful. Panting on slight exertion.

Calcarea carbonica.—Poor condition, now no appetite, now a voracious one. Hair falls off. Rough coat. Enlarged glands. Good during dentition. Abscess in teeth or jaw. Unnatural sweating. Flabbiness.

Calcarea fluorica.—For hard or stony tumors or swellings. Cataract. Varicose veins. Goitre. Bronchocele.

Calendula.—For external application to all bleeding, raw or suppurating parts. Heals injuries quickly.

Cantharis.—Affections of bladder, urinary and generative organs; burning pains; tenderness in affected parts; straining to pass urine; bloody urine; urine passed in small quantities; skin hot. Dog howls from pain.

Carbo vegetabilis.—Windy colic, much discharge of wind. Sluggish, gangrenous, fetid ulcerations or sores. Cold sweats. Distention of abdomen. Foul evacuation with rapid loss of strength. Husky cough with oppressed breathing.

Chamomilla.—A good remedy for minor ills of puppies, diarrhœa, harsh coat, hot nose, etc. Unnatural diminution of milk or it is of poor quality. Retention of milk. Sore teats. Bad tempered, sensitive, high-bred dogs.

Chelidonium.—Useful in liver disease and jaundice, indicated by unnatural yellowness.

Cina.—Useful for the cure of worms—rough

coat, emaciation, yet with unnatural appetite. Grinding of teeth. Goes well with *Sulphur* as an intercurrent.

Colocynth.—Especially useful in painful and severe colic. Diarrhœa follows eating.

Dulcamara.—This remedy is chiefly indicated by its modality "worse in damp weather"—rheumatism, stiffness, diarrhœa, cough, etc., that always come on in cold, damp weather.

Euphrasia.—Useful in affections of the eyes. Eyes red, swollen with yellowish or stringy mucus. Eyes glued together. Ophthalmia, cannot bear the light. Discharge of tears, scalding. Much secretion in nostrils. No appetite but thirsty. Mucus in throat.

Gelsemium.—Strong indications for this remedy are dullness, drowsiness and torpidity.

Watery discharge from nose, sneezing—grippe. Legs and body weak and trembling.

Hepar sulphuris.—Slight injuries suppurate or heal slowly. Swollen glands. To promote suppuration. Unhealthy skin. Mange. Cracks. Fissures. Muffled. Suffocative cough. Pimples and yellowish eruptions. Shivers and seeks the fire or warm place.

Ipecacuanha.—Asthma. Vomiting. Frothy fermenting evacuations in diarrhœa. Suffocative cough.

Kali muriaticum.—A remedy useful in many diseases in their secondary stage. White or grayish mucous discharges. White or grayish phlegm, are guides to its selection.

Kali phosphoricum.—This is especially useful in all states of adynamia, decay, loss of power and general physical breakdown, not caused by old age. Foul ulcers, foul discharges, foul breath. Nervous, no ambition.

Kreosotum.—A remedy for early and rapid decay of the teeth. Teeth dark or black.

Ledum.—A remedy internally and externally for punctured wounds. Also useful for inflammation and swelling of the lower extremities.

Mercurius vivus.—Useful in many affections. Catarrh, sore throat, enlarged glands, bleeding gums, moist oozing eruptions, mange, yellowish appearance, liver diseases, loose cough, slimy evacuations, diarrhœa with much straining, before and after, and unhealthy sweat.

Mercurius corrosivus.—The especial field for the use of this remedy is bloody diarrhœa, dysentery, flux.

Natrum muriaticum.—The especial indications for *Natrum mur.* are *clear*, watery discharges from eyes or nose, that do not excoriate, like the discharges of *Arsen.* White, frothy mucus in mouth. Much sneezing. Seeks open air.

Nux vomica.—A very useful remedy for dogs who are simply "out of condition." Loss of appetite. Piles. Uneasiness after food. Constipation, feces large and hard. Rheumatism. Nose stuffed up.

Opium.—Comatose, drowsy states. Constipation. Body bends backwards. Heat in the head. Nervous system apparently insensible. Slow, heavy breathing. Black evacuations. Lockjaw. Apoplexy.

Phosphorus.—Coat loses all its gloss. Profuse sweats. Hair drops off in patches. General weakness. Evacuations loose.

Phytolacca.—Useful in cancerous affections. Rough, dry sore throat. Induration or suppuration of breast or teats.

Plumbum.—Useful for severe cases of constipation.

Pulsatila.—The dog dislikes heat or warm places and seeks the open air or cool places. Catarrhal affections. Flow of thick yellow or greenish mucus. Useful before and during parturition. Mange.

Rhus toxicodendron. — Very useful in strains and sprains, given internally. Affections of tendons and ligaments; joints. Rheumatism where animal moves and whines from pain, yet apparently is better from motion. Rheumatism brought on by cold and wet. Stiff, rigid back. Itching, inflamed eruptions.

Silicea.—Useful in diseases of long standing. Diseases of bones and periosteum. Fistulous ulcers and sores. Follows *Hepar sulph.*, after abscess has opened. Dog in poor condition, sweats easily on least exertion. Weak.

Sulphur.—Follows well after almost any remedy to complete cure. Useful in skin diseases. Mange. Sluggish abscesses. Coat rough and dirty.

Spongia.—Wheezing, croupy, hollow cough; difficult breathing.

Thuja.—For warts and cauliflower excrescences.

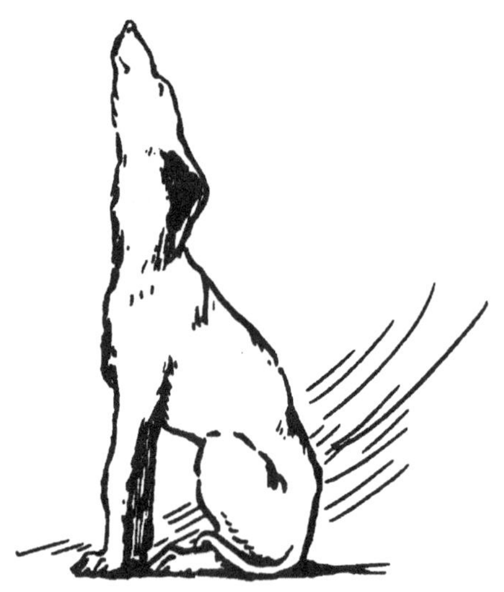

INDEX.

Zeitfracht Medien GmbH
Ferdinand-Jühlke-Straße 7
99095 Erfurt, Deutschland
produktsicherheit@kolibri360.de

Walter Reitz

Die Landschaft in Theodor Storms Novellen

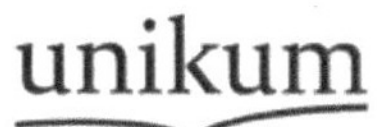

Walter Reitz

Die Landschaft in Theodor Storms Novellen

ISBN/EAN: 9783845724744

Erscheinungsjahr: 2012

Erscheinungsort: Bremen, Deutschland

www.unikum-verlag.de | office@unikum-verlag.de

Bei diesem Titel handelt es sich um den Nachdruck eines historischen, lange vergriffenen Buches. Da elektronische Druckvorlagen für diese Titel nicht existieren, musste auf alte Vorlagen zurückgegriffen werden. Hieraus zwangsläufig resultierende Qualitätsverluste bitten wir zu entschuldigen.